MYSTERIOUS PYRAMIDS

Borobudur:
Ancient Buddhist Temple

Murray "Oak" Tapeta

A Crabtree Crown Book

Crabtree Publishing
crabtreebooks.com

Teaching Tips for Caregivers:

You can help your child learn by encouraging them to read widely, both as a leisure activity and as a way of satisfying their curiosity about the world. Reading helps build a strong foundation in language and literacy skills that will help your child succeed in school. This high-interest book will appeal to all readers in intermediate and middle school grades.

Use the following suggestions to help your child grow as a reader.

- Encourage them to read independently at home.
- Encourage them to practice reading aloud.
- Encourage activities that require reading.
- Establish a regular reading time.
- Have your child ask and answer questions about what they read.

Teaching Tips for Teachers:

Engage students throughout the reading process by asking questions like these.

Before Reading

- Ask, "What do you already know about this topic?"
- Ask, "What do you want to learn about this topic?"

During Reading

- Ask, "What is the author trying to teach you?"
- Ask, "How is this like something you have read or seen before?"
- Ask, "How do the text features (headings, index, etc.) help you understand the topic?"

After Reading

- Ask, "What interesting or fun fact did you learn about Borobudur Temple?"
- Ask, "What questions do you still have about this Buddhist temple? How could you find the answers?"

TABLE OF CONTENTS

A PUZZLE FROM THE PAST

The world is full of mysterious places that hold the secrets of lost **civilizations**. Ancient ruins are like snapshots in time. They provide us with important clues about what life was like long, long ago.

Pyramids usually served as grand burial chambers for royalty or as temples for religious ceremonies or both. These structures exist in various forms around the world, built by civilizations that had little or no contact with one another.

Borobudur is a Buddhist temple built with blocks made of volcanic rock. The tiers of the temple are built in layers of squares and circles. From above, it's shape looks like a mandala, which is a symbol that represents the universe to Buddhists and Hindus.

PYRAMID STYLES

Borobudur is a Buddhist temple built around a hill in the style of a step pyramid. Built in nine platforms, the bottom five layers are squares, the next three layers are circles, and the top layer holds one large dome. Each level is highly decorated featuring wall carvings that tell stories, statues of the Buddha who was the founder of the Buddhist religion, and dome shapes called stupas.

Tikal - Step pyramid

Borobudur - Step pyramid

2600 BCE
Giza

2500 BCE

2100 BCE
Ziggurat of Ur

2000 BCE

900 BCE
Tikal

259 BCE
Qin Emperor

Giza - True pyramid

Ziggurat of Ur - Step pyramid

Teotihuacán - Talud-tablero pyramid

Qin Emperor - Buried flat-topped, step pyramid

BUILT TO IMPRESS!

Why did so many different ancient cultures build similar towering shapes? Relying on the forces of nature, ancient builders learned that the taller you build, the bigger you had to make the base. This helped distribute the weight more toward the bottom so a very tall structure would not topple over.

210 BCE

100 CE

Teotihuacán

450 CE

778 CE

Borobudur

850 CE

900 CE

UNDER THE ASH

From 1811 to 1816, the island of Java in Indonesia was briefly under British control. In 1814, the British Lieutenant-Governor, Sir Thomas Raffles, heard from local people about an incredible monument hidden in the island's dense rainforest. He **commissioned** a team of 200 men on an **expedition** through the jungle to the location he had been given.

After six weeks, the men reached the mountain village of Boro. They slashed and burned trees and bushes. Soon, they discovered piles of ash from an eruption of a nearby volcano. When the ash was cleared away, they found stone figures—thousands of them!

Even though control of Java changed hands back to the Dutch, **excavation** of the site moved forward slowly. It took until 1835 to clear the entire area. What they had unearthed was unlike anything else in the world: the magnificent Borobudur Temple.

A wooden deck was built on Borobudur's main stupa for workers' safety during excavation in the mid 1800s.

JAVA'S HISTORY

Indonesia is made up of thousands of islands—so many, in fact, that no one has an exact count. Some islands are heavily populated and **industrialized**, while others are remote and **uninhabited**. More than half of Indonesia's population lives on the island of Java, one of the largest islands. Java contains the country's most fertile agricultural land. Almost half the people in Indonesia work on the land and much of Java's large population remains rural.

The traditional dance called Bedhaya reflects Java's ancient Buddhist and Hindu influences.

The first Buddhists and Hindus arrived there from India around 100 to 200 CE. These traders, sailors, and religious **scholars** traveled to Indonesia using a maritime trade route between the two countries. By the 1400s, several Buddhist and Hindu kingdoms ruled over large parts of Indonesia. The Dutch came in 1599 and quickly seized control of the spice trade. They **colonized** the islands and enslaved people to farm crops to be exported back to Europe. Indonesia finally achieved independence in 1950.

Many Religions

Islamic traders arrived from India and Persia in the 1200s. As they spread farther inland, they introduced Islam to the country, which grew to become the dominant religion. Today more than 85 percent of Indonesians are Muslim. Less than ten percent are Christian, and even fewer are Buddhist or Hindu. However, the artistic and religious cultures of the Javanese people still reflect the ancient Hindu and Buddhist kingdoms that once ruled there.

TOWERING TEMPLE

Borobudur Temple stands on a hilltop in central Java. This step pyramid was built as a place where **pilgrims** could come to worship. It is truly a marvel. The structure is 115 feet (35 meters) high. The foundation is built in tiers, forming a pyramid shape. Each side of the massive pyramid is 403 feet (123 meters) long. It is the largest Buddhist temple in the world.

The entire temple is built from andesite, a volcanic rock. Researchers estimate that around two million blocks of andesite were used in the construction. The blocks were skillfully cut and assembled using a technique that didn't require **mortar**. The exact dates of construction are not known. But building Borobudur must have lasted for decades. Researchers think it took 70 to 100 years.

In 2006, an earthquake with a 6.2 magnitude struck Java. It caused extreme damage in the nearby cities of Yogyakarta and Prambanan. Borobudur Temple remained intact.

BUDDHIST BUILDERS

What baffles **archaeologists** is that there is no clear record of who created Borobudur Temple. Legends say it was designed by an ancient architect named Gunadharma. Experts estimate that the structure was built between 780 CE and 840 CE. Many believe it was completed during the reign of King Samaratungga of the Syailendra Dynasty.

Not much is known about this time in Javan history. Historians think that rulers in the Syailendra Dynasty helped introduce a religion called Mahayana Buddhism. This type of Buddhism focuses on gaining knowledge and wisdom to reach a level of understanding called enlightenment. The temple seems to have been built to glorify Buddha and to help people achieve enlightenment. During this period, the ruling dynasty erected numerous Buddhist monuments on Java.

THE BUDDHA

Siddhārtha Gautama, commonly referred to as the Buddha, was the founder of Buddhism. He was a wandering teacher who lived in South Asia during the sixth or fifth century BCE. The Buddha taught his followers that the way to enlightenment might take many lifetimes. It depended on following his five moral rules: a person cannot kill, steal, lie, have physical pleasures, and drink alcohol or take drugs.

A JOURNEY TO THE TOP

A popular theory says that Borobudur Temple was built to reflect the three worlds that Buddhists believe make up the universe. Followers who achieve certain moral and mental goals will be reborn into the next higher level.

In Borobudur, the square base at the bottom represents *kamadhatu*, the world of human feelings and desires. The middle level is made up of five square terraces. It represents *rupadhatu*, the world of forms and ideas. Buddhists reach this level after rising above their human desires. The magnificent top level is made up of three round terraces and 72 dome-shaped stupas. It represents *arupadhatu*, the world of formlessness or escape from the physical world. This level is achieved without the body, only the mind. One large stupa sits at the top in the center of the temple.

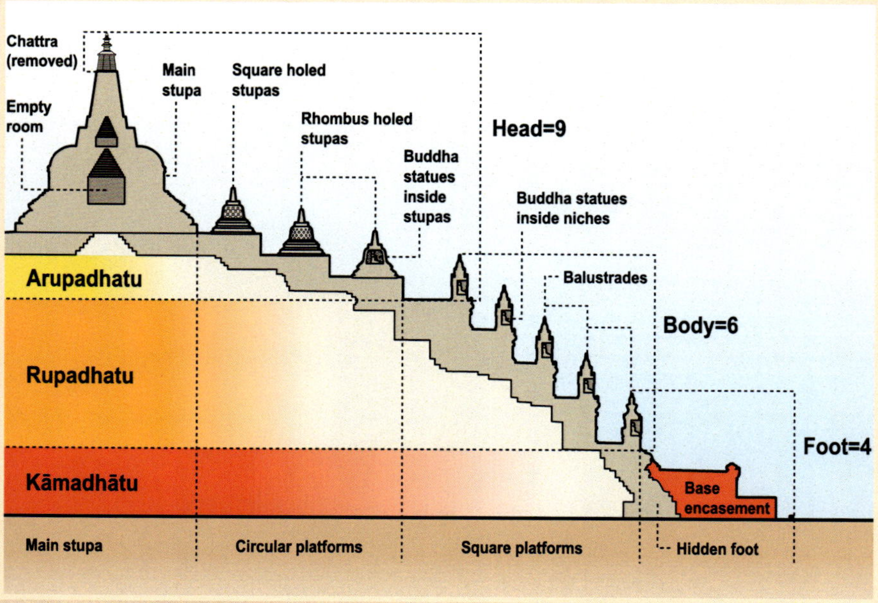

The temple is covered with detailed carvings and statues. More than 2,500 **relief** panels are set into the walls. Their pictures tell the story of the Buddha's life and illustrate sacred stories. They reinforce the Buddha's teachings, which are known as the Dharma or the path of righteousness.

Some carvings show the effects of good and bad actions. For example, they show what happens to people who gossip, rob, or murder. Other carvings focus on kindness and compassion for people and animals.

As you get closer to the top, there is less decoration. The spaces are cleaner and more open. The stupas on the highest level have a lattice design. You can see a statue of Buddha inside each one.

relief image

Buddha inside stupa

There are 100 spouts on the temple shaped like the heads of gods and monsters. They are designed to carry away the water from tropical rainstorms.

MENDUT AND PAWON

To the east of Borobudur Temple are two smaller temples, Mendut Temple and Pawon Temple. The three temples form a straight line. Each one may represent part of the path to enlightenment.

Mendut is the oldest of the three temples and is about 2 miles (3 kilometers) away from Borobudur. Powon lies between Mendut and Bordbudur. The two smaller temples were uncovered after archaeologists finished the excavation of Borobudur. They were restored between 1897 and 1925. These smaller temples also have wall carvings, but unlike Borobudur they both contained small chambers. The large central room in Mendut has three large stone statues. The room in Pawon has only a basin in the center.

PawonTemple

Mendut Temple

PILGRIMS

The Borobudur temple is designed as a **pilgrimage** for Buddhists. It invites people to ascend both physically and spiritually. The idea is to start at the bottom and travel up the path clockwise around the structure. The whole route is more than three miles (five kilometers) long. As they rise higher, followers gain knowledge and wisdom as they view the stories of the Buddha carved into the stone. The large stupa at the center represents the enlightened mind.

Each year, thousands of Buddhist **monks** come to celebrate the holiday of Vesak. They walk silently from Mendut Temple to Borobudur Temple. At night, they release thousands of lanterns into the dark sky.

A BOUNTY OF BUDDHAS

When people think about pyramids, images of gold, jewels, and priceless **artifacts** often come to mind. Borobudur Temple is solid inside with no rooms or spaces to hold such items. It may be that such treasures were never part of the temple. Or it could be that valuable items were taken by thieves long before the temple was rediscovered.

Archaeologists have found traces of gold and brightly colored paint on the relief carvings. Volcanic ash and time seem to have worn them away. The treasures that do remain are the statues of the Buddha. Originally, there were 504 of them. Each one is unique. Their eyes are half-closed in peaceful **meditation**. Their hands are positioned in different mudras, or symbolic gestures.

Before the temple was protected, it was raided by greedy and careless people. They took pieces of the statues. The heads were sold to antique stores or museums. Many of the Buddhas on the site today remain headless.

RESTORING THE TEMPLE

No one is exactly certain why Borobudur Temple was abandoned by the 1500s. It may have been due to a series of volcanic eruptions or to the country's shift away from Hinduism and Buddhism toward Islam. The temples were left buried under volcanic ash and overgrown by vegetation.

The difficult work of restoration on Borobudur Temple began in 1975. To ensure that it will last for many more centuries, over one million stones were moved from the site and set aside like puzzle pieces. They were cleaned and cataloged. The temple was closed to the public for 10 years while it was reinforced and rebuilt. The work cost 25 million dollars.

Mount Merapi is an active volcano that erupts regularly, covering Borobudur with ash. Clearing ash from the temple is a continuous mission.

CONSERVATION

Today, Borobudur Temple is open to the world. It is one of the most popular tourist attractions in Indonesia. More than one million visitors come each year. Watching the sun rise from the top level is a special experience.

However, its popularity as a tourist attraction as well as a place of pilgrimage is one of the things threatening the **preservation** of this ancient site. The stone is in danger of being worn down by too many visitors and damaged by **vandalism**. Volcanic ash and damage from earthquakes also continue to add to the threat of the stone's erosion. Other challenges include **encroaching** development and threats of **terrorism**.

UNESCO is an organization that works to protect unique historical and cultural sites considered important to the entire world. It **spearheaded** the "Save Borobudur" campaign that led to the restoration of the temple in the 1970s. In 1991, Borobudur and the other two temples were officially added to the UNESCO World Heritage List.

The temple was damaged by a terrorist bombing in 1985. Nine stupas and two Buddha statues were destroyed.

GLOSSARY

archaeologists (ahr-kee-AH-luh-juhsts) Scientists who study the distant past by digging up things that people made, used, and left behind

artifacts (AHR-tuh-fakts) Objects made and used by humans in the past, including tools and weapons

civilizations (siv-uh-li-ZAY-shuhnz) Groups of people with their own language and way of life

commissioned (kuh-MISH-uhnd) Order a person to do or make something

colonized (KAH-luh-nighzd) Established control over an area and settlers have been sent to live

encroaching (in-KROHCH-ing) Gradually intruding on someone's space or things

excavation (ek-skuh-VAY-shuhn) The act of digging up or uncovering something

expedition (ek-spuh-DISH-uhn) A voyage or journey taken for a specific purpose

industrialized (in-DUSS-tree-uh-lighzd) Having businesses and factories that produce goods

meditation (med-uh-TAY-shuhn) The act of thinking or focusing on something for a period of time to help relax or for religious purposes

monks (muhngks) Men who live apart from society in a religious community according to strict rules

mortar (MOR-tur) A mixture of lime, sand, water, and cement that is used to hold bricks and stones together

pilgrims (PIL-grimz) People who make a long journey to a scared place for religious reasons

pilgrimage (PIL-gruh-mij) A journey made to visit a shrine or sacred place

preservation (prez-uhr-VAY-shuhn) To preserve, or keep, something in its original state

relief (ri-LEEF) A carving or mold that stands out from the surface

scholar (SKOL-ur) A specialist in a specific field of study

spearheaded (speer-hed-id) Lead a movement or course of action

terrorism (TERR-uh-riz-uhm) The use of fear and unlawful violence to achieve political or religious goals

uninhabited (un-in-HAB-ih-tihd) Having no inhabitants, or people living there

vandalism (VAN-duh-lih-zum) Causing deliberate damage to public or private property

INDEX

QUESTIONS AFTER READING

1. Borobudur Temple is located in the country of _____.
    a. Java
    b. Indonesia
    c. Yogyakarta

2. In 1814, ______ set out to look for Borobudur Temple.
    a. King Samaratungga
    b. archaeologists
    c. Sir Thomas Raffles

3. Andesite is a type of ______.
    a. rock
    b. enlightenment
    c. statue

4. Borobudur is the _______ Buddhist temple.
    a. fanciest b. oldest c. largest

5. Borobudur Temple takes people on a journey from ______.
    a. the mysterious of the past to a bright future
    b. ordinary feelings and desires to spiritual enlightenment
    c. the Syailendra Dynasty to Mahayana Buddhism

Answers: 1. b, 2. c, 3. a, 4. c, 5. b

ABOUT THE AUTHOR

Murray "Oak" Tapeta was born in a toilet-less cabin in Montana. Growing up in the great outdoors, he learned to love trees. He got the nickname "Oak" after climbing to the top of an oak tree when he was only three years old. Oak loves to read and write. He has written a number of books about fascinating, terrible, and gruesome events from the distant past. He prefers spending time in the wilderness with his dog, Birchy.

Author: Murray "Oak" Tapeta

Editor: Kathy Middleton

Proofreader: Crystal Sikkens

Design: Samara Parent and Kathy Walsh

Production coordinator: Candice Campbell

IMAGE CREDITS

Shutterstock: ©Mohammed_Al_Ali, p 7 (second from top); ©Tiwuk Suwantini: p 10–11; ©EDLOSA MEDIA: p 12 (bottom right); ©sugarajfm: p 18 (middle left); ©danviewfinder: p 18 (bottom left); ©Ade Suardika: p 22 (bottom); ©alisyam13: p 22–23; ©Photo Complete: p 26–27; ©Habs Photography: p 28–29

Wikimedia Commons: ©niet bekend / unknown (Fotograaf/photographer). Woodbury & Page (Fotostudio): p 9 (bottom right); ©Gunawan Kartapranata: p 16 (bottom); ©Chainwit.: p 20; ©Indon: p 21 (bottom map)

All other images from Shutterstock

Crabtree Publishing

crabtreebooks.com 800-387-7650

In Canada: We acknowledge the financial support of the Government of Canada through the Canada Book Fund for our publishing activities.

Hardcover 978-1-0398-7280-6
Paperback 978-1-0398-7338-4
Ebook (pdf) 978-1-0398-7393-3
Epub 978-1-0398-7442-8

Published in Canada
Crabtree Publishing
616 Welland Avenue
St. Catharines, Ontario
L2M 5V6

Published in the United States
Crabtree Publishing
347 Fifth Avenue
Suite 1402-145
New York, New York, 10016

Library and Archives Canada Cataloguing in Publication
Available at Library and Archives Canada

Library of Congress Cataloging-in-Publication Data
Available at the Library of Congress

Printed in the U.S.A./CP052026